GETTING TO KNOW
THE U.S. PRESIDENTS

G R O V E R
CLEVELAND

TWENTY-SECOND AND
TWENTY-FOURTH PRESIDENT
1885 - 1889   1893 - 1897

WRITTEN AND ILLUSTRATED BY MIKE VENEZIA

CHILDREN'S PRESS®
A DIVISION OF SCHOLASTIC INC.
NEW YORK   TORONTO   LONDON   AUCKLAND   SYDNEY
MEXICO CITY   NEW DELHI   HONG KONG
DANBURY, CONNECTICUT

Reading Consultant: Nanci R. Vargus, Ed.D., Assistant Professor, School of Education, University of Indianapolis

Historical Consultant: Marc J. Selverstone, Ph.D., Assistant Professor, Miller Center of Public Affairs, University of Virginia

Photographs © 2006: Art Resource, NY/National Portrait Gallery, Smithsonian Institution, Washington, D.C.: 3 (Anders Zorn), 12; Bridgeman Art Library International Ltd., London/New York: 22 (Edward Moran/ Museum of the City of New York), 18 (Fernand Paillet/New-York Historical Society, New York); Corbis Images: 19, 26, 29, 32 (Bettmann), 31; Manlius Historical Society: 8.

Colorist for illustrations: Dave Ludwig

Library of Congress Cataloging-in-Publication Data

Venezia, Mike.
  Grover Cleveland / written and illustrated by Mike Venezia.
      p. cm. — (Getting to know the U.S. presidents)
  ISBN 0-516-22627-4 (lib. bdg.)   0-516-25402-2 (pbk.)
  1. Cleveland, Grover, 1837-1908—Juvenile literature. 2.
Presidents—United States—Biography—Juvenile literature. I. Title.
  E697.V46 2006
  973.8'5'092–dc22
                                        2005012093

1 2 3 4 5 6 7 8 9 10 R 15 14 13 12 11 10 09 08 07 06

A portrait of Grover Cleveland by Anders Zorn (National Portrait Gallery, Smithsonian Institution)

Steven Grover Cleveland was born in Caldwell, New Jersey, on March 18, 1837. As a young man, he stopped using his first name because he thought Grover sounded more important and would be easier for people to remember. Grover Cleveland was the twenty-second and twenty-fourth president of the United States. He was the only president to lose an election and come back four years later to win a second term.

Grover Cleveland first ran for president of the United States in 1884. He seemed to be just the right man to be president. Not only was he honest, fearless, and hard working, but he looked like he could handle any problem that came along. Grover Cleveland was big and powerful and weighed almost 300 pounds. People sometimes called him Big Steve or the Big One. His nieces and nephews even called him Uncle Jumbo!

5

The Cleveland family moved from New Jersey to Fayetteville, New York, when Grover was four years old. Grover's father was a minister. He always looked for towns with lots of churchgoers so he could support his growing family.

Grover had five sisters and three brothers. He was a hard-working boy. He babysat his younger brothers and sisters and did all kinds of odd jobs to make money.

Grover did take time off to play pranks on townspeople, though. Years later, when he was president, Grover returned to Fayetteville to give a speech. He admitted that as a boy, he had taken people's front gates off their fences. By then, of course, everyone had forgiven him.

Grover started his education in a little one-room schoolhouse. His father also taught him religious studies at home. Reverend Cleveland was pretty strict. He expected his children to behave like adults. He taught Grover the importance of being responsible, honest, and loyal.

This is how Fayetteville looked when Grover Cleveland was growing up there in the mid-1800s.

When Grover was older, he went to Fayetteville Academy. He hoped to go on to college, but he never made it. When his father became ill, Grover dropped out of school to help make extra money for his family. Grover took a job in a general store for fifty dollars a year. Sadly, a short time later, Reverend Cleveland died, when Grover was just sixteen.

Grover decided he would give up his college plans and support his family full time. He headed off to the big city of Cleveland, Ohio. Grover thought there would be lots of opportunities there, plus he liked the name! When Grover stopped along the way in Buffalo, New York, however, he decided to stay there. Grover had an uncle in Buffalo who helped him get a job as a clerk, or helper, in a law office.

Grover decided then he would like to be a lawyer. In the 1800s, a person didn't need a college education to be a lawyer. Grover could study and work with attorneys until he learned enough to pass his law exam.

Grover worked long, hard hours studying. One night, the lawyers he worked for forgot Grover was in the office studying, and locked him inside when they went home!

A photograph of Grover Cleveland as a young man

In 1858, Grover Cleveland passed his law exam at the age of twenty-two. Soon the hard-working Grover became known as an excellent lawyer. He was even asked to take an important position as the county's assistant district attorney.

During the years when Grover was building a successful career, the Civil War started. Grover never served in the army, though. He managed to stay out of the war so he could keep working and sending money to his family.

In 1870, Grover was elected sheriff of Erie County. After three years, he decided to go back to being a lawyer. He had done such a good job as sheriff, however, that in 1881, he was asked to run for mayor of Buffalo.

Grover Cleveland belonged to the Democratic political party. When party leaders asked Grover to run for mayor, Buffalo's city government was filled with crooked politicians. For years these politicians had taken bribes, rigged elections, and stolen money from the city treasury. The citizens of Buffalo were fed up with their government leaders. They wanted someone who could run their city in an honest way. Grover won the election and became mayor of Buffalo in 1882.

Grover had promised to get rid of crooked
government workers. The dishonest workers
were outraged, but there was little they
could do. The citizens of Buffalo loved their
new mayor.

Grover did such a good job as mayor of Buffalo, he was soon asked to run for governor of New York State. It seemed like the whole state was filled with dishonest government workers, too. Grover was elected governor in November 1882 and took office in 1883. He worked harder than ever to stop anything that seemed the least bit wasteful or dishonest.

Grover Cleveland's reputation as a strong and honest governor was spreading all over

the country. In 1884, Democratic leaders asked him to run for president of the United States. Grover agreed and ran against the Republican Party candidate, James G. Blaine. It was a close race, but Grover won. Grover Cleveland had gone from being an ordinary everyday lawyer to president of the United States in a little over three years!

A portrait of Frances Folsom Cleveland by Fernand Paillet

When Grover Cleveland started his new job, he was still a bachelor. That didn't last for long, though. In 1886, Grover married Frances Folsom. Grover Cleveland was the only president to get married in the White House.

Grover was twenty-seven years older than Frances. Many years before, Frances's father had been Grover's law partner. When Frances was eleven, her father was killed in an accident. Grover generously offered to help take care of the Folsom family.

A political cartoon from 1886 showing the wedding of Grover Cleveland and Frances Folsom

After Frances grew up and graduated from college, Grover fell in love with her. Even though newspapers had a good time making fun of the old bachelor and the young bride, everyone loved the First Lady. Frances was very pretty and had a great sense of humor. Grover and Frances ended up having five children.

As president, Grover Cleveland governed the same way he had governed as mayor and governor. He didn't put up with any nonsense at all. President Cleveland warned government employees to work as hard as they could or they would be fired.

When a president turns down a bill presented to him by Congress, it's called a veto. During his first term, President Cleveland vetoed a record-breaking 414 bills that he thought were wasteful or dishonest.

Many of President Cleveland's vetoes
turned down requests from congressmen for
money to help Civil War veterans. The
president wasn't against helping veterans,
but he found out many dishonest soldiers had
been making up stories about their injuries.
President Cleveland refused to give out any
money that would benefit crooked politicians
or ex-soldiers.

On October 28, 1886, President Cleveland gave a speech at the unveiling of the Statue of Liberty in New York Harbor. The statue was a gift from the people of France. It had been shipped from France in 350 pieces and then reassembled when it got to the United States.

This painting by Edward Moran shows the Statue of Liberty on the day it was unveiled, October 28, 1886.

The Statue of Liberty celebrated the freedom and liberties the United States had offered its citizens for the past 100 years. It became a welcome symbol for hundreds of thousands of immigrants who came to the United States looking for a better life.

President Cleveland was always concerned about the economy of the United States. He knew a strong economy would keep workers happy and big businesses running smoothly.

When Grover ran for reelection in 1888, against Benjamin Harrison, the economy was in pretty good shape. But Harrison's supporters raised lots of money to get their man elected, and Harrison won by a very narrow margin.

During President Harrison's four-year term, things started going wrong with the economy. President Harrison believed in raising a tax called a tariff. The tariff made prices higher and made it harder for average working people to live.

President Harrison and his supporters also wasted a lot of money. They gave even more money to Civil War veterans, whether they deserved it or not. These were exactly the kinds of things Grover Cleveland tried to avoid.

Grover couldn't stand sitting by while the United States headed for trouble. In 1892, he decided to run for president again.

The program from President Cleveland's 1893 inauguration

Grover Cleveland ran against Benjamin Harrison again. This time, Grover won.

Frances Cleveland had had a feeling her husband would become president again. Before leaving the White House at the end of Grover's first term, Frances told the servants and staff to keep everything in perfect shape.

The First Lady said she and Grover would be returning in four years. Everyone had a good laugh over the prediction, but Frances wasn't joking.

As soon as President Cleveland returned to office, he faced a serious national money problem called a depression. A depression is a period of time when banks and other businesses close and workers lose their jobs.

The depression caused serious problems for President Cleveland and the people of the United States. Even lucky workers who didn't lose their jobs had to take salary cuts. When employees at the Pullman railroad car company in Illinois had their salaries cut, they became angry and refused to work. Soon railroad workers across the country went on strike, too.

President Cleveland sent these troops to Illinois to break up the
Pullman Railroad Strike in 1894.

Even though President Cleveland supported
the country's workers, he felt they had gone
too far this time. The railroad strike was
preventing the U.S. mail from being delivered!

The president sent federal troops to force
workers back to their jobs, even though
the governor of Illinois didn't want him to
do so. Unfortunately, a violent riot broke
out. Many workers were injured, and some
were even killed.

President Cleveland had angered workers across the country by his decision to force railroad employees back to their jobs. But when Grover Cleveland thought he was doing the right thing, he didn't care who he offended.

Once, President Cleveland became angry with Great Britain. He was convinced the British were trying to grab land away from Venezuela, a country in South America. Grover Cleveland felt this action broke the rules of the Monroe Doctrine, a document that protected South America from unfriendly European countries.

Grover Cleveland in the early 1890s

President Cleveland was so angry that he threatened to go to war with Britain unless it dealt more fairly with Venezuela. Some people felt the president made a brave move, but others felt he acted in a reckless and dangerous way by risking war.

Grover Cleveland and his family in the early 1900s

Grover Cleveland was honest and hard working. He wanted to have a lot of control over Congress, and broke all records using his veto power. Unfortunately, Grover Cleveland had few good ideas about how to fix the depression or how to solve the difficulties between workers and their bosses. By the time Grover Cleveland left his job as president in 1897, everyone blamed him for the country's problems.

Grover Cleveland went back to being a lawyer again after he left the White House. He lived out a happy life with his family in Princeton, New Jersey, where he died in 1908.